curious thoughts

curious thoughts

max cryer

HarperCollins*Publishers*

National Library of New Zealand Cataloguing-in-Publication Data

Curious thoughts / Max Cryer.
ISBN 1-86950-451-8
1. Aphorisms and apothegms. 2. English wit and humor.
I. Cryer, Max.
398.921—dc 21

First published 2002
HarperCollins*Publishers (New Zealand) Limited*
P.O. Box 1, Auckland

ISBN 1 86950 451 8

Designed by Alice Bell
Typeset by Graeme Leather
Printed by Editions Book Production, Hong Kong

contents

introduction

When I was a student of English literature, I quickly developed a liking for the aphorism—'pithy sayings which outline a general truth'. (The fact that such witty sayings are also quite correctly called 'maxims' didn't do any harm.)

Years later, when my language sessions started featuring regularly on National Radio, I worked with a succession of very quick-witted people: Brian Edwards, Gary McCormick, John Campbell, and Kim Hill. The information I broadcast is often quite heavy on the research. To form a bridge back to the more cheerful Saturday morning approach of my hosts, I developed the habit of ending my segment with a light-hearted one-liner, usually language based.

I know you've heard this before . . . but quite truly, people started to say, 'Why don't you put those lines into a book?' So I did.

MAX CRYER
NOVEMBER 2002

pun-ishment

A pessimist's blood type
is always B-negative.

A Freudian slip is when you say
one thing but mean your mother.

Some men need a mistress
just to break the monogamy.

A book on voyeurism
could be called a peeping tome.

Banning the bra
was something of a flop.

Condoms should be used
on every conceivable occasion.

The dog was called Carpenter because
he did little jobs around the house.

If an Oriental person is spun
around on his feet several times,
he may become disorientated.

A reckless driver is not the same
as a wreckless driver.

On a taxidermist's window:
'We really know our stuff.'

Santa Claus weeds his garden
with a hoe, hoe, hoe.

The Energizer Bunny was arrested
and charged with battery.

Potatoes cooked by nuclear power
will be fission chips.

A man's home is his castle,
in a manor of speaking.

A hangover is the
wrath of grapes.

He likes to make pottery,
but to me it's just kiln time.

Working in the blanket factory
was a good job, until it folded.

Practise safe eating—
always use condiments.

Corduroy pillows are
making headlines.

Dancing cheek-to-cheek
—a form of floor play.

The name Pavlov somehow
rings a bell . . .

Without geometry,
life is pointless.

Dreaming in colour is a pigment
of your imagination.

The sailor who went to sleep on his
watch must have been very small.

Spaghetti should not be cooked too long—about 25 centimetres is enough for most people.

Reading while sunbathing makes you well red.

In a podiatrist's office:
Time wounds all heels.

On the day they paid off the mortgage, their baby was born—so they named her Bernadette.

They called their second-hand car Opportunity because they could always hear it knocking.

animals

When hens squawk, you are listening to fowl language.

Many of the qualities you love to see in people are exhibited full time by dogs.

Joe Bennett

The hens were very interested when
they heard that the mayor was
going to lay a foundation stone.

He who feeds the pelicans,
fills the bill.

A cat doesn't have as many lives
as a frog, which croaks every night.

The early bird gets the worm,
but the second mouse gets the cheese.

When it rains,
sheep don't seem to shrink.

If a giraffe gets wet feet
it develops a sore throat . . .
but not until a week later.

Dogs laugh with their tails.

When betting on horses,
they seem to win one day,
and lose the next. So maybe
just bet on alternate days!

less is more—
food and dieting

A successful diet is the triumph
of mind over platter.

People planning to go on a diet
are wishful shrinkers.

Diets are for people who are
thick and tired of it.

A dieter's great ambition is to be
weighed and found wanting.

A diet should help you
go out of your weigh.

If you want to grow thinner,
diminish your dinner.

People who go on a diet and say
it doesn't work are poor losers.

It may be time to diet when sitting down
causes your width to double.

Cannibals don't eat clowns,
because they taste funny.

You'll know your sausages
have been genetically modified
when they walk to the cupboard
and get their own tomato sauce.

A cheese can last for 50 years
and still be going strong.

An obese person is
a fat accompli.

Hymn to tomato sauce:
First with vigour shake the bottle,
None will come, and then a lot'll.

the demon drink

When intoxicated, a person feels
sophisticated—but can't pronounce it.

If the doctor says it's OK to have
the odd drink, just take glasses one,
three, and five, and leave the rest.

One tequila, two tequila,
three tequila . . . floor.

Alcohol puts the wreck
into recreation.

Beauty is in the eye
of the beer holder.

He had hangover eyes—
they felt like unpeeled kiwi fruit.

A stiff drink is the only good reason
to get up each afternoon.

Here's to champagne—the drink divine,
Which makes us forget out troubles,
It's made of a dollar's worth of wine
And ten dollars' worth of bubbles.

leisure

Bicycle riding is supposed to help a weight problem—yet it increases appetite!

Exercise for one minute and you add one minute to your life span. So, at age 85, you can spend an additional five months in a rest home.

Cross-country skiing is wonderful,
but it's best to start with a small country.

If your figure and your health need
attention and you pay to join a
health session at the gymnasium . . .
remember that for it to be effective
you have to show up now and then.

I get plenty of exercise . . . I watch
sport on telly three times a week.

Never do card tricks for the
group you play poker with.

A truly wise man never plays
leapfrog with a unicorn.

Unkind comment on a famous sportsman:
He has the speed of a racehorse,
the strength of a draught horse
and the brain of a rocking horse.

'Reality television' may be
an oxymoron—it certainly
involves some kind of a moron.

Modern pop music is noise
with copyright.

Book review of the biography of a
very young show-biz star:

'From cradle to shave.'

Early to bed and early to rise
describes people who don't care
about television.

Very short newspaper cricket report:
'Rain, no game.'

Rugby starts from the grassroots up,
not from the corporate box down.

Isaac Sola

Jonah Lomu—a steamroller
wearing shorts.

Name for a private pleasure boat:
CIRRHOSIS OF THE RIVER.

A yacht which hasn't been
paid for is a floating debt.

There are many people who
drop a line to the fish but
don't hear back from them.

If all the year were holidays, to sport
would be as tedious as to work.

Shakespeare

The difference between drama
and melodrama is that in drama
the leading lady throws the man
over. In melodrama she throws him
over a cliff.

Theatre sometimes holds a mirror
up to life and sometimes a keyhole.

An effective speech has a good beginning
and a good ending, close together.

Applause when a speaker is introduced = faith.
Applause in the middle of a speech = hope.
Applause at the end = charity.

Fashion is a form of ugliness so great
that we have to alter it every six months.

Oscar Wilde

Suggested sequel for SILENCE OF
THE LAMBS—SHUT UP EWES.

Pat Elphistone

After a cancelled season,
the actors were all work and no play.

politics

Oppositions don't win elections
—governments lose them.

A politician who complains about the media
is like a sailor who complains about the sea.

In politics, if you want anything said,
ask a man; if you want anything done,
ask a woman.

Margaret Thatcher

A person with a good voice,
a confident vocabulary and a microphone
is likely to develop into a political party.

It is wiser to judge a politician's stature
from his chin upwards, than from
his shoulders down.

My opinion about Western civilisation
is that it would be a very good idea.

Mahatma Gandhi

Every taxpayer has a huge staff on
his payroll—the entire government.

When a politician promises to speak straight
from the shoulder one can't help wishing
his talk originated a little higher up.

PRO is the opposite of CON, but progress
isn't the opposite of congress.

Mob rule can sometimes
become democrazy.

Politicians and babies' nappies have one
thing in common: they should both be
changed regularly—and for the same reason.

Someone has to back down
when the public gets its back up.

Democracy evolved because everyone wants other people to share the blame.

The word 'politics' breaks down into 'poli' (meaning many) and 'tics' (meaning bloodsucking parasites). Surely not!

Capitalism is man exploiting man; socialism is the other way around.

insults

He is the sort of man other men would follow
—but only out of curiosity.

He would be out of his depth
in a paddling pool.

The man has delusions of adequacy.

Some people are alive only
because it's illegal to kill them.

God must love stupid people;
He made so many.

Concentration level? Well, to be
kind, he's been working with
glue too much.

If someone says they're sorry they
forgot to come to your party,
simply exclaim that nobody
noticed they weren't there.

I'm trying to imagine you
with a personality.

This person is depriving a village
somewhere of its idiot.

He brings a lot of joy to a room
—whenever he leaves it.

He is cleverly disguised
as a responsible adult.

I've had a wonderful evening
—but this wasn't it.

Earth is full. Go home.

When you see two people talking and
one looks bored, the other one's him.

It takes fewer muscles to smile than
to frown—and even fewer still to
ignore someone completely.

He doesn't even qualify for
the 'fun' in 'dysfunctional'.

He has a great future ahead—
but has missed a lot of it already.

He was a self-made man—
but had left work rather early.

The gates are down and the lights
are flashing but the train never arrives.

It's hard to believe he beat 100,000
other sperm to get to the egg.

The wheel is turning but
the mouse is dead.

It's good to see people with
get-up-and-go, especially if they're
visitors who've stayed too long.

the ego

He was like a cock who thought
the sun had risen to hear him crow.

George Eliot

An egotist usually talks about himself
so much that there is no time left
for you to talk about yourself.

Only one thing can keep growing
without nourishment—an ego.

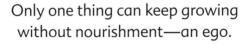

the ego

When I want your opinion,
I'll give it to you.

My husband and I divorced over
religious differences—he thought
he was God and I didn't.

It's very pleasing to meet a man
who says exactly what he thinks
—as long as he agrees with you.

One good thing about egotists—
they don't talk about other people.

Too much patting on someone's
back can have the unexpected effect
of causing their head to swell.

Some people are born great and
others achieve greatness—
but some just grate.

the ego

I intend to live forever.
So far, so good!

Galileo was wrong.
The world revolves around me!

Yes, you are unique;
but so is everyone else.

When two egotists meet,
it's an I for an I.

from the
school room

Ancient Egyptians
wrote in hydraulics.

Hebrew slaves made unleavened
bread which means bread without
any ingredients.

Solomon had 300 wives
and 500 porcupines.

Some people can tell the time by
looking at the sun, but other people
find it hard to read the numbers.

Francis Drake used a 100-foot
clipper to circumcise the world.

Socrates was sent to trial
and then condommed to death.

In the ancient Olympic games,
Greeks ran races, jumped, and
hurled biscuits.

Noah's wife was Joan of Ark.

The climate of the Sarah Desert
is so severe that all the inhabitants
have to live somewhere else.

The ten commandments were
found on Mount Cyanide.

Socrates was a famous Greek teacher
who went around giving people advice.
They killed him.

Hitler shot himself
in the bonker.

Joan of Arc was tied to a
steak and burned.

Sir Walter Raleigh is famous because he
invented cigarettes and started smoking.

William Shakespeare wrote tragedies,
comedies and hysterectomies. All of them
were written in Islamic pentameter.

Milton wrote PARADISE LOST. Then his wife died and he wrote PARADISE REGAINED.

Benjamin Franklin died in 1790 and is still dead.

Charles Darwin wrote THE ORGAN OF THE SPECIES and Madam Curie discovered the radio.

Handel was half German, half Italian, and half English. He was very large.

Beethoven was deaf so he wrote very loud music. Beethoven expired in 1827 and later died.

In the nineteenth century people stopped reproducing by hand and started reproducing by machine.

Johann Sebastian Bach wrote a great many musical compositions and had a large number of children. In between he practised on an old spinster up in his attic.

Socrates died from an overdose of wedlock. After his death, his career suffered a dramatic decline.

New York is a busy city with high buildings
and people crowded together, that's why
it is known as The Concrete Jandal.

A sobering thought about Noah,
Samson, Moses and Jesus:
they did it all without a car.

from the school room

This is Ernie, he's the slowest boy in
our class—and I'm not far behind him!

School exam instruction:
Correct the use of apostrophe's.

The Bible begins with
the Book of Guinness.

money

The difficulty with many people's incomes
is that they budget 30% on shelter,
30% on clothing, 40% on food and
20% on amusement.

Socialists believe making profit is a vice.
I consider the real vice is making losses.

Sir Winston Churchill

A daughter will be pleased that her fiancé
has a certain something, but her father
would prefer he had something certain.

It is true that only two things in life
are certain—death and taxes, but it's a
pity they don't usually come in that order.

The person who says diamonds shouldn't be worn in daylight, doesn't own any.

'Money can't bring happiness.' Funny how it's usually rich people who say that.

At the end of the financial year the female of the species is less deadly than the mail.

business

There are two kinds of people who can change white to black—painters and lawyers.

The woman who started a bonsai workshop was so successful, she had to move into smaller premises.

Beware when buying second-hand cars —it can be hard to drive a bargain.

Noah's ark was built by amateurs:
the T<small>ITANIC</small> was built by professionals.

Name of second-hand shop:
Junk and Disorderly.

Does an insurance broker deal
in things that are broken?

The paint-factory worker who fell in a vat
came out overcome with emulsion.

On a fence:
Salesmen welcome!
Dog food is expensive.

In the front yard of a funeral home:
Drive carefully. We'll wait.

A barrister can be debarred
and a priest can be defrocked,
but it's slightly different when
a hairdresser is distressed.

Bills travel through the mail at
twice the speed that payments do.

A professional knife sharpener's
business relies on things being dull.

It is quite legitimate for a bus driver
to tell you where to get off.

Lawyers who win a court case tell
their clients, 'We won.' But if they don't
win, they tell the clients, 'You lost.'

Job creation in a 'new market' economy:

Hiring someone
to insult customers.

It can be worrying that the man who invests all your money is called a broker.

She was a good receptionist
as good receptionists go, and as
good receptionists go, she went.

Hairdressers are deceptively friendly
people who attack your hair with
scissors and a pack of lies.

Elena Lappin

I wouldn't call the place I work an office
—it's Hell with fluorescent lighting.

I thought I wanted a career, but it turned
out all I wanted was a salary.

If you like buying things marked down,
be careful you don't buy a whole escalator.

A bald man is bound to have faith in a
hair restorer which comes with a free comb.

If you're dealing with a broker,
try to ensure it's stock, not pawn.

Sign on a plumber's truck:

You don't have to sleep
with a drip tonight.

Back of a truck:
Crime doesn't pay.
Often, trucking doesn't either.

Name for a holiday-district septic-tank cleaner:
The Wizard of Ooze.

It could be alarming that a
doctor's workplace is customarily
called a 'practice'.

A trendy description helps sell something:
try labelling a used trampoline as a
solar-powered tanning bed.

Sign in workplace:

Caution—you may be paid
what you're worth.

Sign in an optometrist's window:
If you don't see anything you want,
then you've come to the right place.

If fired from their jobs,
would an electrician be de-lighted;
an out-of-work musician de-noted;
a fashion model de-posed ;
and a dry cleaner de-pressed?

computer literate?

computer literate?

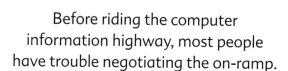

Before riding the computer
information highway, most people
have trouble negotiating the on-ramp.

Sign on monitor screen:

You have reached the end of
the internet. There is nothing more
to know. Go back to the beginning.

A person who is tired of playing with the internet is surf-bored.

Who spends a lot of time in front of a computer? A 'mouse potato'.

To err is human, but to really foul things up requires a computer.

Computer programmers
don't byte, they nibble a bit.

A married computer operator
has a quizzical view of two
particular keys—Ctrl and Esc.

Most children have an invisible
friend. So do most adults—theirs
is called Technical Support.

computer literate?

Definition of an intellectually challenged person:

When the computer instruction says
'Press Any Key' the person looks
for the key marked 'Any'.

Home is where you hang your @

sickness and health

Hay fever can be positive or negative
—sometimes the eyes have it,
sometimes the nose.

A hospital is where people who
get run down wind up.

There are sometimes
four stages to sickness:
(1) ill; (2) pill; (3) bill; (4) will.

Medicine advertising can be so
attractive that people who have
nothing wrong with them feel
they're missing out on something.

When you are well your feet
run and your nose smells, but when
you are sick, your feet smell
and your nose runs.

battle of the sexes

Wedding telegram:

Twenty-five years ago you went
to bed with a dummy.
Now history is repeating itself.

Cynical man:

If it's too tight, a wedding ring
cuts off your circulation, and even
when it fits—it still does.

Disgruntled woman:
I baked my boyfriend a pie,
but he left me for a tart.

Some cynics say a married man
can have one wife too many
and not be a bigamist.

Hell hath no fury like the
lawyer of a woman scorned.

The neighbours called the woman
at the end of the street 'Doe'—
because every buck stops there.

The sea of matrimony is one
in which it has often proven
difficult to keep heads above water.

If some men can be got up onto the
moon, why aren't they ALL sent there?

Husbands are very like fires;
they go out if not attended to.

Zsa Zsa Gabor

It's very seldom you'll hear a man
say, 'Does this shirt make me look fat?'

A husband is what's left of a lover
after the nerve has been extracted.

Question: How do you spell marriage?

Answer: M-i-r-a-g-e.

She was the kind of woman who wasn't satisfied with being Queen Bee —she wanted to be Queen A.

She had many of the qualities of a fireside poker, except that a poker is occasionally warm.

Definition given by a man:

Marriage is a relationship in which one person is always right and the other is a husband.

Women believe they live seven years longer than men—because that's how long it takes to clear up the mess the men leave.

My recipe for a successful marriage:
don't forget your wife's birthday. I never
forget whats-'er-name's birthday.

Men are from Mars and women
are from Venus but they still need
spacecraft in between.

Fay Weldon

Woman: a rag; a bone;
a hank of hair.
Man: a brag; a groan,
a bag of air.

Last night I killed my husband
Stretched on the parquet flooring,
I was loath to take his life
But I had to stop him snoring.

Arthur or Martha

If English had gender nouns,
a web page would be female
—because it's always being hit on.

The traditional description 'hourglass'
is still a good way to describe the female
figure—because given time, all the weight
goes to the bottom.

A photocopier is perceived as
a non-human but female object
—because once turned off, it takes
a long time to warm up again.

Even in a man, kidneys would logically
be classified as female organs—because
they always go to the lavatory in pairs.

A male gynaecologist is like a
mechanic who's never owned a car.

Women must do everything twice
as well as men to be thought half
as good. Luckily, this is not difficult.

Charlotte Whitton

An unoccupied shoe suggests maleness
—because it's usually unpolished and
has its tongue hanging out.

When women are depressed they
either eat or go shopping.
Men invade another country.

Elayne Boosler

A mammogram does not involve
putting your breast in an envelope
and sending it to someone.

If men can run the world, why can't
they stop wearing neckties?

Tautology: a statement in which
one half simply repeats the meaning
of the other half, e.g. 'working mother'.

A tyre must be a male object
—it is often over-inflated and
then goes bald.

Hammers share some characteristics
with men—they have not developed
or evolved over the last 5000 years,
but they are still handy to have around.

If knives had a gender, the Swiss Army
knife would be male—because although
it is designed for multiple capabilities,
most of its time is spent opening bottles.

ageing
disgracefully

It was once a nice firm chin—but now
the firm has taken on a couple of partners.

Growing old is unavoidable,
growing up is optional.

Always go to your friends' funerals—
otherwise they won't come to yours.

Yogi Berra

A woman: 'I'm forty-five.' Pause.
'OK, I'm forty-five plus GST.'

Edie Baker

From the back of a truck:

People never really grow up—
they just learn how to act in public.

Middle-aged people are medically
recommended to do exercises every
day, followed by a light siesta—
daily dozen and daily dozing.

Your life is slowing down when there are only a few commandments left that you are capable of breaking.

Senior policeman to another: 'Have you noticed how young the criminals look these days?'

This computer is like my father— old, slow, and not much memory.

Some middle-aged people take up gymnasium sessions, just so they can enjoy hearing heavy breathing again.

In rare cases a pendulous stomach can be a minor asset—it hangs so low it conceals flabby thighs.

As soon as a person feels 'mature', someone calls them 'old'—and the two things don't feel the same.

You're getting on in years
when your heartache is caused by
your heart and not by your children.

It's some sort of a sign when
your birthday cake has so many
candles that the fire alarms go off.

Middle age creeps up on you
—like underwear does.

Middle age is when a person
who was a human dynamo
starts to have ignition trouble.

Time is a great healer,
but no beauty specialist.

Many a man continues to think
that he's as good as he never was.

The usual definition of 'middle age' is that it's about ten years older than you are.

Middle age is when the middle grows faster than the age.

The midlife brain is a wonderful organ— it starts the moment you get up in the morning and does not stop until you get to the office.

The hardest years in a woman's life
are between ten and seventy.

Helen Hayes (at 73)

Once you're over the hill,
you pick up speed.

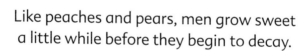

Like peaches and pears, men grow sweet
a little while before they begin to decay.

O. W. Holmes

You are getting near superannuation if:

- The Prime Minister is younger than you are.

- You tell people you have backache, but they don't make coarse remarks about it any more.

- Your knees buckle and your belt won't.

You are getting near superannuation if:

- You find yourself chasing women but can't remember why.

- An exercise workout really means a good brisk sit.

- Doing without sex is less worry than doing without your glasses.

You are getting near superannuation if:

- 'Getting a little action' really means the prune juice has had some effect.

- You can sing along with the tunes they play in lifts.

- Bran doesn't taste so bad.

You are getting near superannuation if:

- Everything you have either hurts or doesn't work.

- Someone tells you to pull in your stomach when you already have.

You are getting near superannuation if:

- Your back goes out more than you do.

- The destiny which shaped your ends
  has also ended your shape.

- You get winded playing cards.

You are getting near superannuation if:

- You can still chase girls, but only if they're going downhill.

- The end of the rainbow turns out not to have gold, just a pot.

- When the phone rings on Saturday night you hope it isn't for you.

You are getting near superannuation if:

- Your broad mind and narrow waist have swapped places.

- Faced with two temptations you choose the one that will get you home earlier.

- You feel like the morning after without having been anywhere the night before.

You are getting near superannuation if:

- A night out is followed by a day in.

- Dialling London wears you out.

- First you forget names, then forget faces, then forget to pull your zip up, then forget to pull it down . . .

You are getting near superannuation if:

- You sit in a rocking chair and can't get it going.

- You look at the menu before looking at the waitress.

- The only thing you exercise is caution.

You know you're growing old
At least that's how I find it
When you not only are
But also do not mind it!

Len Deighton

the meaning
of life

God is egalitarian—
you're no safer in first class.

Today is the tomorrow you
worried about yesterday.

The best thing about being 100
years old would be that there's
very little peer pressure.

Atheism is a non-prophet organisation.

Man is said to have evolved
from monkeys and apes . . . but
we still have monkeys and apes.

Don't take life too seriously;
you won't get out alive.

I can reach for excellence—
but perfection is God's business.

Michael J. Fox

I try to take one day at a time,
but sometimes several attack me at once.

If you can't be a good example,
then you'll just have to be a
horrible warning.

Experience is something you don't
get until just after you need it.

Success always occurs in private,
and failure in full view.

Well, this day was a total
waste of make-up.

Older men declare war, but it is youth
who must fight and die.

President Herbert Hoover, 1944

I could make ends meet if only
they stopped moving the ends.

God's surname is not known—
but it's very unlikely to be Zilla.

A 'conclusion' is what you decide
when you're tired of thinking about it.

All the world's a stage—and some people are desperately unrehearsed.

He who hesitates is not only lost, but may also be many kilometres away from the next motorway exit.

For every action there is an equal and opposite criticism.

Integrity is doing the right thing
when nobody's watching.

A pessimist is a person who
prefers to be seasick throughout
the entire voyage of life.

I started out with nothing and
still have most of it left.

A 'holy war' is the great
oxymoron of our time.

Gordon McLauchlan

Hypocrisy is the Vaseline
of political intercourse.

Evita Bezuidenhout, South African entertainer

He who dies with the most
toys is nonetheless dead.

faces

Their faces were as expressionless
as a row of empty mailboxes.

He had one of those faces that
had worn out four bodies.

Some people have a perpetual
expression of smelling something
burning on the stove.

Her face was like royalty
being given a tour and suddenly
coming across a smelly drain.

It was one of those faces
like guava jelly that hasn't set
properly and is about to run.

human nature

There's only one thing more
exasperating than a person
who thinks he knows it all—
and that's a person who
actually does know it all.

I've heard so much about you
—I'd like to hear your side of the story.

I am very much in favour of
long walks—especially when people
I don't like take them.

People will ignore almost any form
of public behaviour except seeing
someone in the supermarket express
queue with 13 items instead of 12.

Some people regard the truth
as so precious that they use it
with great economy.

One of the important factors
in a relationship is whether
you boil at different degrees.

When starting a relationship, remember,
new shoes always hurt for a while.

Three people can keep a secret
only if two of them are dead.

Benjamin Franklin

When some people make speeches,
they think deep noises from the throat
equal important messages from the brain.

If at first you don't succeed . . . blame
someone else and then seek counselling.

Adolescence is the period when children believe they will never grow up as stupid as their parents.

A man in a suit says, 'There are one billion stars in the universe,' and we believe him. A sign says, 'Wet paint, don't touch,' and we have to feel the paint to make sure.

Conscience is a faculty of the mind which, when you are doing wrong, tells you you're about to be caught.

People often aren't listening to you—until you make a mistake.

You can't fool all of the people all of the time, but it's strange how many keep trying to do it.

Getting on your high horse
is a good way of riding for a fall.

A clear conscience is often
the sign of a bad memory.

Generally speaking, people survive
adversity better than they
survive prosperity.

Nothing is as good as
it seemed beforehand.

George Eliot

When you get what you
want you don't want it.

Marilyn Monroe

The word 'wish' always applies
to something you haven't got.

Fear the goat from the front,
the horse from behind,
and man from all sides.

Russian proverb

Inside every older person
is a younger person wondering
what the hell happened.

Stupidity doesn't count as a handicap
—so you can't park in this space.

The problem with being punctual is that
no one is ever there to appreciate it.

People who are late are usually
of a happier nature than those
who have been waiting for them.

Nobody can make you feel
inferior without your permission.

Eleanor Roosevelt

If anything is worth doing, surely it
would have been done already . . .

If at first you don't succeed,
there's always next year.

If at first you don't succeed,
destroy all evidence that you tried.

I'm not tense, just terribly,
terribly alert.

Most people want either
less corruption, or more chance
to participate in its benefits.

Why waste time reliving the past when you can waste time worrying about the future?

A young mother can find great difficulty in accepting that other people have perfect babies too.

Perseverance can be defined as a
strong will; obstinacy as a strong won't.

A conscience is what hurts when
all your other parts feel good.

The human race seems to
have improved everything except
human nature.

whoever said English
was logical?

Infants have no choice about infancy—
do adults have a choice about adultery?

Horrific means it was horrible—
so does terrific mean it was terrible?

Electricity comes from electrons—
so does morality comes from morons?

One tooth, several teeth.
But not one phone booth, several beeth.

There is no egg in eggplant, no ham in
hamburger, and quicksand works slowly.

The weather was hot as hell on Monday
and cold as hell on Tuesday!

If he plays the piano, call him a pianist—
but if he races cars, don't call him a racist.

We must polish the Polish furniture.

If you have ever been tongue-tied; a tower
of strength; hoodwinked; in a pickle; have
knitted your brows; or slept not a wink
—you are quoting Shakespeare.

If you say you wound a bandage around
a wound . . . pronounce it carefully.

The caretaker said the bins were full
—he had to refuse any more refuse.

Sweetmeats are candy, not meat,
and sweetbreads are meat, not bread.
But at least sweetmeats are sweet!

Insurance claims are sometimes invalid
if made by an invalid.

In German, 'Strauss' means 'ostrich' or
'small bouquet'—so in English, the famous
composer Johann Strauss would be called
Johnny Ostrich or Johnny Posy.

At a recital, performers play;
but at a play, performers recite.

The boat's crew had a row
about who was to row.

People from Poland are called Poles
. . . but it might not be wise to call
someone from Holland a Hole.

A group of sheep is called a mob
. . . but better not call the person who
looks after them a mobster.

If you get rid of all your odds and ends
except one . . . is it an odd or an end?

Chinese are said to be inscrutable . . .
which must make everyone else scrutable.

When 'listless' you lack energy.
But on a good day, try telling
someone you're 'list'.

After several washes, permanent
indelible marking pens sometimes
turn out to be delible.

I'm not indifferent . . . but that
doesn't make me different.

One hundred potatoes could be described
as quite a lot . . . or quite a few.

A vegetarian eats vegetables, so should
we be careful of a humanitarian?

Strange that a wise guy is the
opposite of a wise man.

It is rarely said of a woman
that she is a spring chicken.

I thought I had to fill in the form,
but a supervisor told me to fill it OUT.

Beware of the word 'cleave'—it means
to split apart and also to stick together.

When an alarm clock switches on
its bell we say it has gone OFF!

They're called tugboats, but they usually PUSH other vessels.

Two English words have all the vowels in the right order: abstemious and facetious.

The word 'invisibility' has only one vowel—five times!

It's usually called a TV set—
even though you only get one.

You can comb through the annals
of history—but, curiously, you can't
comb through one annal at a time.

The soldier decided to desert
his dessert in the desert.

If your lost property has vanished into
thin air; you refuse to budge an inch;
are given short shrift; insist on fair play;
but finish up laughing yourself into stitches
—you are quoting Shakespeare.

She saw the tear in her beautiful
dress and shed a tear.

Boxing rings are square!

whoever said English was logical?

You will never see a horseful
carriage or a strapful gown.

When a house is burning UP,
we say it is burning DOWN.

To start my watch going, I wind it up,
and to bring a meeting to an end,
I wind it up.

whoever said English was logical?

A slim person and a fat person
are quite different—but a slim chance
and a fat chance are the same.

If you suspect foul play; lie low;
feel bloody-minded; stony-hearted;
with your teeth set on edge—
you are quoting Shakespeare.

It doesn't matter what the
room temperature is . . .
it is always 'room temperature'.

'Look' and 'see' mean almost
the same thing, so it's strange
that 'overlook' and 'oversee'
are virtually opposites.

whoever said English was logical?

If you play fast and loose;
have too much of a good thing;
but suffer from green-eyed jealousy;
and then become a laughing stock
—you are quoting Shakespeare.

It's a poor mind that can only think
of one way to spell a word.

Although a goose and her
husband are geese,
a moose and his wife
are not meese.

When stars come out
they are VISIBLE.
When light bulbs GO OUT
everything is invisible.

definitions . . .

Accountant—someone hired to explain
that you didn't make the money you did.

Balderdash—one way of describing
a rapidly receding hairline.

Chillenge—running down to the
letter box in winter, without a coat.

Claustrophobia—
being frightened of Santa.

Consciousness—the annoying time
in between naps.

Cuberty—the stage reached by
teenagers when their parents
seem square.

Depression—reaching rock bottom
then starting to dig.

Dilate—to live as long as
the Queen Mother did.

Dreadlocks—a fear
of opening the door.

Economics—telling you things you've
known all your life but in a language
you can't understand.

Economist—a person who tells you
what to do with your money after
you've done something else with it.

Esplanade—the attempt to give
an explanation while drunk.

Giraffiti—vandalism
spray-painted VERY high.

Glibido—all talk and no action
from a would-be seducer.

Gossip—someone with a
great sense of rumour.

Heck—where the people go
who don't believe in Gosh.

Hipatitis—a new disease among
trendies who've spent too long
aiming for terminal coolness.

Inflation—when you are paying out twice as much in taxes as you used to earn in wages.

Inocu-latte—the desperate person's way of getting a coffee fix intravenously.

Intaxication—the thrill of receiving a refund from the tax department.

Irritainment—new description for senseless television programmes.

Lame duck—a person whose goose has been cooked.

Market research—knowing the answer you want, but having to frame the question that will produce it.

Meanness—box containing two batteries
and a note saying 'Gift not included'.

Modesty—a man who has caught
a really huge fish carrying it home
through a back road.

Negligent—absent-mindedly answering
the door in your nightie.

Obtainable data—the papers left clean
after you spilled coffee over the others.

Optimist—someone who thinks
there will be good strawberries at
the bottom of the punnet.

Overactive imagination—an
indication of underactive reality.

Punctuality—the art of guessing
how late the others will be.

Smorgasbord—being tired of buffets
full of Scandinavian food.

Stress—when you wake up screaming
and realise you weren't asleep.

Synonym—a word you use when you can't spell the one you want to use.

Tact—the art of being able to advise someone to lose 10 kilos without ever mentioning the word FAT.

Tax reform—taking taxes off things that have been taxed in the past, then putting tax on things that weren't taxed before.

Thermomater—a device for bringing compatible couples together, by matching their body heat.

Voice jail—the communications nightmare created by automated phone systems.

. . . and other
word explanations

Biography is the story
of a person's life.
Autobiography is the story
of a person's car.

Flatulence is NOT an emergency
vehicle that picks you up after you've
been run over by a steamroller.

Ladies of easy virtue grouped together:
an essay of trollops, an anthology of pros,
a jam of tarts, or a fanfare of strumpets.

To 'look' means to see something:
to 'overlook' means you pretend
not to see it.

'Move to a strategic position'
usually means 'retreat'.

'Moving in cycles' is a dignified way
of saying 'running round in circles'.

'In my experience'
often means 'once'.

'It has always been acknowledged'
usually means 'I didn't look
up any references'.

'It is generally believed' often
means 'I heard two people say so'.

'According to statistical analysis'
is one way of saying 'there is a rumour'.

'A statistically orientated significance
projection' usually means 'a wild guess'.

modern life

Survival in the 21st century:

Keep your back to the wall,
your ear to the ground,
your shoulder to the wheel,
your nose to the grindstone,
both feet on the ground
and a level head,
but still look for the silver lining.

If Barbie is so popular,
why do you have to buy her friends?

Advertising is the science of
arresting the human intelligence
long enough to get money from it.

Stephen Leacock

When it comes to car crashes, it's not
who's right that counts, it's who's left.

The moon used to be an inspiration
to poets, songwriters and lovers. It will
be sad if it becomes just another airport.

The first piece of luggage that
comes out on an airport carousel
seldom seems to belong to anyone.

In a bookstore, don't ask
where the self-help books are—they
might tell you to find them on your own.

Stealing a good idea is called
plagiarism, stealing a whole lot
of ideas is called research.

Hire purchase for furniture is one way
of ensuring you eventually own antiques.

Answerphone message:
This is the refrigerator—speak slowly
and I'll stick your message to myself
with one of those magnets.

Note on desk:
Out of my mind.
Back in five minutes.

I think, therefore I am overqualified.

The colder the X-ray table, the more
of your body is required on it.

A microphone can be a great help
amplifying a speaker's voice—
but not necessarily their ideas.

Helpful label in T-shirt:

Made of: cotton and other stuff.
Wash: when dirty.

Change is inevitable—
except from those parking-meter
money machines.

In a one-way street at least you can
only get bumped in the rear.

'Rush hour' is an oxymoron: because
the traffic is mostly going very slowly.

You never really learn to swear
until you learn to drive.

If all the feeble-minded people
were locked up, who would
write the TV commercial jingles?

Exercise in uselessness:
Announcing over the PA that
a hearing aid has been found.

First sentence of a modern fairy tale:

Once upon a time there were
three bears—a mother bear,
a father bear, and a baby bear
from a previous relationship.

Ask not for whom the telephone
bell tolls . . . if thou art in the shower,
it always tolls for thee.

curious
thoughts

Many an argument is sound.
Just sound.

Since we are assured that witches
still exist, do they ride around on
vacuum cleaners?

There is no thrill quite like being
in the dark and treading on a step
that isn't there.

In winter the days get later earlier.

Black eyes don't come free—
they have to be fought for.

To a reluctant housewife 'dust'
is a noun but very seldom a verb.

What was the best thing
BEFORE sliced bread?

If everything's coming your way,
it probably means you're in the wrong lane.

Some mistakes are too much
fun to make only once.

How long a minute is depends
on which side of the bathroom
door you are.

He who laughs last,
thinks slowest.

Being empty-headed doesn't
mean you're open-minded.

It is a waste of time
answering an anonymous letter.

Yogi Berra

Flying through clouds, everyone
hopes the silver lining they've
heard about doesn't turn out
to be another plane flying
in the opposite direction.

A sponge cake could be
quite different from a cake
which was sponged.

Two memorable non sequiturs:

I never go to a play
unless I've seen it before.

Reported by Roger Hall

I never go to a hairdresser
—they always make such
a mess of me.

Sophia Loren

Memorable mixed metaphors:
Give him enough rope
to shoot himself in the foot.

It must not be made to seem
that I am milking the gravy train.

Reported by Gordon McLauchlan

A rule of physics points out that things
expand in heat and contract in cold.
Which must be why the days
are longer in summer.

A critic is a man with
no legs teaching running.

Channing Pollock

If a tortoise doesn't have a shell,
is it homeless or naked?

A person who is grossly ignorant
must be 144 times worse than
someone who is just plain ignorant.

If love is blind, it's strange that
beautiful lingerie is so popular.

If a mute person swears, does his
mother wash his hands with soap?

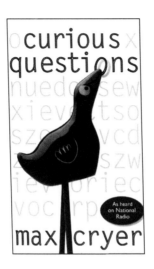

CURIOUS QUESTIONS is a goldmine of information
about the way New Zealanders use the English
language. Perfect reading for reference or pleasure.

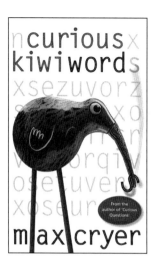

From 'hangi' to 'gumboots', from 'give it heaps' to 'pack a sad', CURIOUS KIWI WORDS is chock-full of fascinating information for Kiwis and tourists alike.

HarperCollinsPublishers